THE GOSPEL PROJECT

HEARING GOD'S WORD

Immersed in His Story

George Guthrie

LifeWay Press®
Nashville, Tennessee

Item: 005737302
ISBN: 978-1-4300-4139-9
Dewey decimal classification number: 220.07
Subject heading: BIBLE — STUDY \ BIBLE — USE \ GOD — WILL

Eric Geiger
Vice President, Church Resources

Ed Stetzer
General Editor

Trevin Wax
Managing Editor

Faith Whatley
Director, Adult Ministry

Philip Nation
Director, Adult Ministry Publishing

Angela Reed
Content Editor

We believe that the Bible has God for its author; salvation for its end; and truth, without any mixture of error, for its matter and that all Scripture is totally true and trustworthy. To review LifeWay's doctrinal guideline, please visit *www.lifeway.com/doctrinalguideline.*

Unless otherwise noted, all Scripture quotations are taken from the Holman Christian Standard Bible®, copyright 1999, 2000, 2002, 2003, 2009 by Holman Bible Publishers. Used by permission.

For ordering or inquiries, visit *www.lifeway.com;* write LifeWay Small Groups; One LifeWay Plaza; Nashville, TN 37234-0152; or call toll free (800) 458-2772.

Printed in the United States of America.

Adult Ministry Publishing
LifeWay Church Resources
One LifeWay Plaza
Nashville, Tennessee 37234-0152

TABLE OF CONTENTS

ABOUT THE GOSPEL PROJECT

Some people see the Bible as a collection of stories with morals for life application. But it's so much more. Sure, the Bible has some stories in it, but it's also full of poetry, history, codes of law and civilization, songs, prophecy, letters—even a love letter. When you tie it all together, something remarkable happens. A story is revealed. One story. The story of redemption through Jesus. This is *The Gospel Project.*

When we begin to see the Bible as the story of redemption through Jesus Christ, God's plan to rescue the world from sin and death, our perspective changes. We no longer look primarily for what the Bible says about us but instead see what it tells us about God and what He has done. After all, it's the gospel that saves us, and when we encounter Jesus in the pages of Scripture, the gospel works on us, transforming us into His image. *We become God's gospel project.*

ABOUT THE WRITERS

George Guthrie serves as the Benjamin W. Perry Professor of Bible and Senior Fellow in the Ryan Center for Biblical Studies at Union University in Jackson, Tennessee. He has written numerous books and articles on study of the Bible, including *Read the Bible for Life: Your Guide to Understanding and Living God's Word.* He is married to Pat, and they have two children, Joshua and Anna.

Barry Cram adapted this material for use with small groups.

HOW TO USE THIS STUDY

Welcome to *The Gospel Project*, a gospel-centered small-group study that dives deep into the things of God, lifts up Jesus, focuses on the grand story of Scripture, and drives participants to be on mission. This small-group Bible study provides opportunities to study the Bible and to encounter the living Christ. *The Gospel Project* provides you with tools and resources to purposefully study God's Word and to grow in the faith and knowledge of God's Son. And what's more, you can do so in the company of others, encouraging and building up one another. Here are some things to remember that will help you maximize the usefulness of this resource:

GATHER A GROUP. We grow in the faith best in community with other believers, as we love, encourage, correct, and challenge one another. The life of a disciple of Christ was never meant to be lived alone, in isolation.

PRAY. Pray regularly for your group members.

PREPARE. This resource includes the Bible study content, three devotionals, and discussion questions for each session. Work through the session and devotionals in preparation for each group session. Take notes and record your own questions. Also consider the follow-up questions so you are ready to participate in and add to the discussion, bringing up your own notes and questions where appropriate.

RESOURCE YOURSELF. Make good use of the additional resources available on the Web at *www.gospelproject.com/additionalresources* and search for this specific title. Download a podcast. Read a blog post. Be intentional about learning from others in the faith. For tips on how to better lead groups or additional ideas for leading this Bible study, visit: *www.ministrygrid.com/web/thegospelproject.*

GROUP TIME. Gather together with your group to discuss the session and devotional content. Work through the follow-up questions and your own questions. Discuss the material and the implications for the lives of believers and the mission to which we have been called.

OVERFLOW. Remember, *The Gospel Project* is not just a Bible study. *We* are the project. The gospel is working on us. Don't let your preparation time be simply about the content. Let the truths of God's Word soak in as you study. Let God work on your heart first, and then pray that He will change the hearts of the other people in your group.

THE GOSPEL PROJECT

Session 1

Valuing God's Word

We all need to hear the word of God more than
God needs any of us to defend it. [1]

KEVIN DEYOUNG

INDIVIDUAL STUDY

The Rosetta Stone, which is dated about two centuries before the birth of Christ, was uncovered in 1799 and displays a decree made by a council of Egyptian priests concerning 13-year-old ruler Ptolemy V. The decree was inscribed on the stone in three languages—hieroglyphics, demotic, and Greek.

This parallel display proved an immensely valuable linguistic key. Prior to the stone's discovery, the ability to read and write hieroglyphics—a script made up of pictures—had been lost in the mists of human history. Scholars of the early 19th century were able to use the Greek writing on the stone to unlock the mysteries of Egyptian hieroglyphics.

The Rosetta Stone served as a key for unlocking the mystery of ancient Egyptian life. In the same way, God's Word serves as a key for unlocking the lost truths of our lives. Our God is a communicator by nature. He has spoken, revealing truth about Himself, why we human beings are here on earth, and what He expects of us. But sin has a way of distorting our ability to understand God and His Word—making His way "lost in translation," so to speak. And perpetual ignorance of His Word can keep us lost in more ways than one.

What are some places or resources people turn to in order to understand the best way to live?

How has a lack of knowledge of God's Word brought hardship to your life?

Reading the Bible is an important part of the Christian life. In this session, we will see that reading God's Word helps us grow in our relationship with God as we learn more about Him and His ways. We also read God's Word in order to know how to live. Living on mission for God's kingdom, we must obey His commands and guard ourselves from sin. God's Word is to be a source of joy, since in His Word we come to know the story of our world and we meet the Savior—Jesus Christ.

Throughout the week engage these daily study sections on your own. Each of these examines the different aspects of valuing God's Word. There are three daily readings to prepare you before your group meets for this session. Interact with the Scriptures, and be ready to interact with your group.

To Know Him Better

Among the psalms, Psalm 119 stands out as a beautiful, poetic celebration of God's Word and its many benefits. This week, we're going to consider the first sixteen verses of this psalm, noting several ways we benefit from engaging God's Word on a regular basis. Each day, we will read different verses from this passage and then dig into some truths we discover in these words.

> ² Happy are those who keep His decrees
> and seek Him with all their heart.
>
> ⁷ I will praise You with a sincere heart
> when I learn Your righteous judgments.
> ⁸ I will keep Your statutes;
> never abandon me.
>
> ¹⁰ I have sought You with all my heart;
> don't let me wander from Your commands.
> PSALM 119:2, 7-8, 10

We read the Word of God so that we can know Him better. The Bible is God's love letter to His people, through which He communicates His heart and vision for our lives. When a couple starts dating, they spend time together—sharing meals, talking long walks, writing notes to each other. All of these activities are different ways of sharing life with the purpose of getting to know each other better.

Discuss a time when words and conversation helped you develop a relationship with another person.

Similarly, we grow in our relationship with God as we come to know Him through Scripture. Where else would we learn about the character of God as holy, or about the kindness and grace of God, or about the acts of salvation He has carried out for people? Apart from the words of the Bible, we would know nothing about many particulars of God's nature, His purposes, His actions, or His plans for the future. The Bible is the primary means by which we can get to know God better.

Apart from the words of Scripture, we could not know God Himself. We would have no understanding of His message of salvation accomplished through Jesus Christ. In fact, Jesus is the ultimate way God revealed Himself to us (Heb. 1:1-2). In the person of Jesus, God Himself stepped onto the earth to show us what He is like. It is through Jesus that God invites us to become His sons and daughters (John 1:12). We would know little to nothing about Jesus apart from the words of the Bible, and Jesus introduces us to the Father.

The Bible both establishes the beginning of our relationship with God and helps facilitate its growth. Notice that early in Psalm 119, seeking or knowing God is often associated with knowing the words of God. Verse 2 says, "Happy are those who keep His decrees and seek Him with all their heart." In this verse the keeping of God's decrees goes hand-in-hand with seeking God with all of one's heart.

Psalm 119:7-8 says, "I will praise You with a sincere heart when I learn Your righteous judgments. I will keep Your statutes; never abandon me." Do you see the connection between praise and righteous judgments? Praising God with a sincere heart flows from being engaged with God's "righteous judgments." When we understand more of God's righteous character, His words lead us to praise.

"I have sought You with all my heart; don't let me wander from Your commands" (Psalm 119:10). A heart conditioned by a close relationship with God becomes a basis for continuing in the ways of God. In other words, as we grow in our understanding and living of God's Word, that truth shapes our hearts to love God more. Our hearts are transformed, and God's ways are preserved in our hearts.

Loving God and loving the Word of God are mutually reinforcing. They reciprocate each other. If you want to know God, grow in your understanding of His Word. If you want to endure in following His Word, a strong relationship with God is the foundation for a life well lived. Read the Word of God on a regular basis, and expect your heart to be opened to the living God.

> **Describe an experience when you grew spiritually because of the presence of God's Word in your life.**

2 To Live According to His Will

> [1] How happy are those whose way is blameless,
> who live according to the LORD's instruction!
>
> [3] They do nothing wrong;
> they follow His ways.
> [4] You have commanded that Your precepts
> be diligently kept.
> [5] If only my ways were committed
> to keeping Your statutes!
> [6] Then I would not be ashamed
> when I think about all Your commands.
>
> [9] How can a young man keep his way pure?
> By keeping Your word.
>
> [11] I have treasured Your word in my heart
> so that I may not sin against You.
> **PSALM 119:1, 3-6, 9, 11**

We read the Scriptures to understand God's will. In the first verses of Psalm 119, the "commands" and "instruction" of the Lord are front and center—"How happy are those whose way is blameless, who live according to the LORD's instruction." If you want a "happy" life that is "blameless," live by the Lord's instruction (119:1). The godly person follows God's "ways" (119:3) and keeps His "precepts" (119:4), His "statutes" (119:5), and His "word" (119:9).

How does this picture of a "happy life" differ from what the world would offer you?

Foundationally, our lives are shaped by how we think. That's why the Lord's "instruction" is vital for a life well lived. Through His Word, He teaches us the truth about life and the paths we should take. He shows us the patterns that should characterize our actions, attitudes, and relationships. He guards us by forbidding certain paths.

Simply, God's Word shows us the way we should go and the ways we shouldn't go. It trains us in the ways of God and provides an ever-present guide for living. How can we live under the constant influence and power of the Lord's Word? By treasuring His Word in our hearts (119:11).

> What is something that you "treasure," or hide away somewhere, because it is so valuable to you? How does the value you give this treasure compare to the value you place on God's Word in your life?

The Dead Sea Scrolls are the greatest archaeological discovery of the past century. In 1946, Bedouin shepherds discovered a cave near the Dead Sea containing large clay jars that housed ancient manuscripts. Over the next decade, more caves were found. These caves had been used by a first-century community of Jews to hide hundreds of scrolls. Before computers and hard drives, smart phones and apps, these scrolls were literally hidden away to preserve them. They were hidden because they were treasured.

We might ask ourselves how careful we are with the Word of God. Have we packed it away like treasure in our hearts? Do we attend to it as valuable, storing it up in our memories in a way that the Word can be brought before our hearts at a moment's notice by the Spirit of the living God?

The psalmist suggested that this is a key to living well: "I have treasured Your word in my heart so that I may not sin against You" (119:11). Staying on the right track in life may seem a monumental task at times. We need supernatural help, and one of the resources God has given us is His good Word. In fact, John Stott noted, "It is no exaggeration to say that without Scripture a Christian life is impossible."[2]

Significantly, God's Word trains us to live in line with the purposes of God. God's primary, twin purposes for us are to love Him and to advance His mission and glory on the earth. We love God by living according to His commands (Deut. 6:4-9). We bring Him glory by advancing His mission in the world. So our living according to the ways of God is key to our living out the purpose of God for our lives.

3 Because It Gives Us Joy

¹ How happy are those whose way is blameless,
who live according to the LORD's instruction!
² Happy are those who keep His decrees
and seek Him with all their heart.

¹³ With my lips I proclaim
all the judgments from Your mouth.
¹⁴ I rejoice in the way revealed by Your decrees
as much as in all riches.
¹⁵ I will meditate on Your precepts
and think about Your ways.
¹⁶ I will delight in Your statutes;
I will not forget Your word.
PSALM 119:1-2, 13-16

We've seen how we read the Bible to know God better and to know how to obey His will. But in speaking of obedience, we must never think of the Word of God as simply a list of rules for living, as if they were laws of drudgery. Rather, we read the Bible because it gives us joy.

We all need joy! What is something in your life that recently gave you joy? Encouraging words from a friend? A wonderful line from a book? An enthusiastic hug from a toddler? A letter or note from someone you love? The completion of an especially difficult project at work? Good news from far away? As the list suggests, many joy-prompts come in the form of words, and the author of Psalm 119 reflected on the Word of God as producing joy.

Make a list of the benefits of following God's Word. What are some ways we can make sure our Bible reading is joyful and not a chore?

People in our culture long for happiness. In 2008, around four thousand books on the topic of "happiness" were published.[3] Only God can bring ultimate happiness to a human being. Who is "happy" according to verses 1-2? Those who "live according to the LORD's instruction," those who "keep His decrees and seek Him" wholeheartedly.

The greatest example of joy through obedience, of course, is Jesus Himself. Hebrews 12:1b-2 says, "Let us run with endurance the race that lies before us, keeping our eyes on Jesus, the source and perfecter of our faith, who for the joy that lay before Him endured a cross and despised the shame and has sat down at the right hand of God's throne."

Notice Jesus' positive and negative actions here. Negatively, He "despised" the shame of the cross. In the ancient world, there was no more shameful death than crucifixion. To even mention a cross or crucifixion in some cultural contexts was considered rude because it brought such gruesome images to mind. The word translated "despised" here means "to look down on something with contempt" or "to treat something as of little value." So, in effect, Jesus "shamed" the shame of the cross, treating it as of little significance.

We too need to put the costs of our obedience in perspective. To live by God's ways in the world demands countercultural living and thinking. Following God's will may have great personal cost, and it may even involve persecution and suffering. But we can "despise" the cost of discipleship in the sense of putting such costs in eternal perspective. When we live according to God's will and follow Jesus' example of obedience, we walk the same path that Jesus walked.

Positively, Jesus endured in obedience to the Father, and the Word of God gives us a firm foundation, sure guidance, from which to endure in living according to God's ways in the world. And notice the payoff we see in Jesus' example—joy! He despised the cost and endured in obedience, not out of some sense of dutiful drudgery but for the joy that was coming.

Psalm 119:14 reads, "I rejoice in the way revealed by Your decrees as much as in all riches," and verse 16 speaks of the "delight" the psalmist had in God's Word. The word translated "rejoice" in verse 14 can refer to enjoying something, to be made glad, or to find pleasure in something. We grow in our delight in God's Word as we grow in our delight in God Himself.

In what ways can we help ourselves and others understand that the path of obedience to God is the path of true joy?

How might part of your struggle to be happy in life relate to your struggle to be obedient to God?

GROUP STUDY

Warm Up

As we began this session, we read about the Rosetta Stone and how it served as a key for unlocking the mystery of hieroglyphics. Likewise, the Bible, God's Word, "unlocks" the correct way to "read" all of life. God is the Creator of all things who knows the purpose for all things. He has spoken, revealing truth about Himself, why we human beings are here on earth, and what God expects of us.

Use the space below to write an encouraging note to a spouse, child, parent, or friend. After the group completes their notes of encouragement, answer the following questions:

What would the recipient of your note be able to know about you through your words?

What are some attributes of God we would not know apart from His revelation of Himself in His Word?

In Psalm 119:1-16, what are some attitudes the psalmist has toward God's Word? What kind of appeals does the psalmist make to God about His Word?

Discussion

There's life and there's energy in the Bible.
We read other books while this Book reads us.[4]
ADRIAN ROGERS

During this time you will have an opportunity to discuss what God revealed to you during the week. Listed below are some of the questions from your daily reading assignments. They will guide your small-group discussion.

1. What are some places or resources people turn to in order to understand the best way to live? How has a lack of knowledge of God's Word brought hardship to your life?

2. Discuss a time when words and conversation helped you develop a relationship with another person.

3. Describe an experience when you grew spiritually because of the presence of God's Word in your life.

4. What is something that you "treasure," or hide away somewhere, because it is so valuable to you? How does the value you give this treasure compare to the value you place on God's Word in your life?

5. Make a list of the benefits of following God's Word. What are some ways we can make sure our Bible reading is joyful and not a chore?

6. In what ways can we help ourselves and others understand that the path of obedience to God is the path of true joy?

7. How might part of your struggle to be happy in life relate to your struggle to be obedient to God?

Conclusion

What is the Bible else but a letter of God Almighty addressed
to His creatures, in which letter we hear the voice of
God, and behold the heart of our heavenly Father?[5]

AUGUSTINE

If we want to hear God, then knowing the Bible is where we must start. But the point is not merely that we know the Bible, but that we choose and determine to live by it. This week's passage reiterated how we should respond to God's Word—to walk in it, keep it, learn it, and obey it. And if we choose to obey God's Word, then we have, at some point, realized that it is better for us to obey than to disobey.

Spend some time praying this for yourself and for your group:

"God, please teach me to value Your Word more tomorrow than
I do today. Help me plan my days better so I can read Your Word.
As you reveal Yourself in Scripture, help me know You more.
Show me the path to find delight in Your Word. Amen."

1. Kevin DeYoung, *Taking God at His Word* (Wheaton: Crossway, 2014), 25.
2. John R. W. Stott, *Understanding the Bible* (Grand Rapids: Zondervan, 2011) [eBook].
3. Julia Baird, "Is Happiness Overrated?" *Newsweek* [online], 24 September 2009 [cited 3 September 2014]. Available from the Internet: *www.newsweek.com*.
4. Adrian Rogers, *What Every Christian Ought to Know* (Nashville: B&H, 2012), 23.
5. Augustine, quoted in *The Divine Unity of Scripture*, by Adolph Saphir (London: Hodder and Stoughton, 1892), 81
6. George Müller, quoted in "Quotes," *GeorgeMuller.org* [online; cited 10 September 2014]. Available from the Internet: *www.georgemuller.org*.

The vigor of our spiritual life will be in exact proportion to the place held by the Bible in our life and thoughts. [6]

GEORGE MÜLLER (1805-1898)

NOTES

Session 2

Focusing on Biblical Perspective

The Bible is not just a library of religious books; it is the inspired
and authoritative Word, a unified message from God to us. [1]

MARK STRAUSS

INDIVIDUAL STUDY

With the advent of digital photography, more and more people have taken up photography as a hobby. Today, anyone can take pictures with their smart phone or a compact camera. Many amateur photographers will spend money on a nice camera, but to be a serious or professional photographer, they will need to invest in all kinds of camera equipment to take their hobby to the next level.

Consider the DSLR (Digital Single-Lens Reflex Camera). In the world of serious photography, the lenses constitute the greatest investment. Those who are serious about photography know that a good camera can cost anywhere from several hundred to several thousand dollars. But the real investment for top-level photography lies in the quality and variety of lenses a person purchases.

Quality is a key. Exceptionally well-made lenses make for top-quality pictures. But variety is needed. Some lenses are suited best for close-ups, others for low-lighting, others for portraits, and still others for zooming in on wildlife or capturing panoramic landscapes.

> **What are some examples of lenses and their purposes (glasses, photography, etc.)?**

When we think about reading the Bible, the "lenses" we use as we read are very important. In this session, we will discuss three basic, "high-quality" lenses in our toolkit for reading, understanding, and living the Bible effectively. Each of these ways of reading the Bible shines a particular light on our reading and provides a rich experience of hearing God in the pages of His Word.

First, we are to read the Bible in light of the Bible, which means we shouldn't isolate one text from the rest of Scripture. Second, we are to read the Bible as one great story that points us to Jesus Christ. Finally, we are to read the Bible in community with other believers so we can be strengthened for the mission God has given us.

Throughout the week engage these daily study sections on your own. Each section examines the different lenses through which we should read the Bible. There are three daily readings to prepare you before your group meets for this session. Interact with the Scriptures, and be ready to interact with your group.

1 Read the Bible in Light of the Bible

We need to read the Bible through the lens of the Bible itself. This might seem like circular thinking, but it is not. When we think about the whole canon of Scripture (that is, all of the books of the Bible together), we are talking about a body of literature, a wonderful, fascinating collection of "books" that spans centuries.

Speaking of the Old Testament era, Hebrews 1:1 tells us that "Long ago God spoke to the fathers by the prophets at different times and in different ways," and yet it was the one true God doing the speaking. Writers of the New Testament understood this truth, and they often read Old Testament passages in light of other passages. (A good example is found in Hebrews 1:5-14.) Today, we have the advantage of reading the whole of Scripture, both Old and New Testaments.

At times, the Old Testament gives us vitally important background information for what is going on in the New Testament. For instance, you cannot really understand Paul's words in 1 Corinthians 5:7, where he calls Christ "our Passover," unless you know the story of the Passover in Exodus 12.

At other times, New Testament passages give us perspective on passages from the Old Testament. For example, consider Jesus' words in Matthew 5:38-42:

> 38 "You have heard that it was said, An eye for an eye and a tooth for a tooth. 39 But I tell you, don't resist an evildoer. On the contrary, if anyone slaps you on your right cheek, turn the other to him also. 40 As for the one who wants to sue you and take away your shirt, let him have your coat as well. 41 And if anyone forces you to go one mile, go with him two. 42 Give to the one who asks you, and don't turn away from the one who wants to borrow from you.
> MATTHEW 5:38-42

In verse 38, Jesus alludes to Exodus 21:23-25 and Deuteronomy 19:21. "An eye for an eye" was a common legal code in the ancient Near East, called *lex talionis*. In a positive sense, it limited punishments to make sure they were in line with the offense. Regardless of class, it recognized that every person was valuable and his or her person should be respected. But the law could be twisted to justify revenge.

We should read this Old Testament law in light of Jesus' teaching about the kingdom. He did not negate the law but rather qualified justice with mercy. The kingdom way, in other words, is to extend mercy even when you have legal recourse for exacting revenge.

The other examples Jesus gave, turning the other cheek and offering a person your clothing, make a similar point. Radical kingdom living means drawing attention to the kingdom by not getting what is coming to you, whether revenge or respect or even basic necessities of life. The point is that the Old Testament laws at times are put in perspective by the New Testament teaching of Jesus and the apostles.

How do you think a Christian can determine when to turn away from legal recourse today?

What are some ways we can evaluate our motives when confronted with difficult situations involving our person, honor, or possessions?

We need to know the whole of Scripture to shed light on difficult questions and situations— to understand and act appropriately based on what God is saying to us in the Word. And the first place we should look for more light is in the Bible itself.

What are some tools we might use to help ourselves and others read the Bible in light of the Bible?

2 Read the Bible in Light of Christ

There is a second "high-quality lens" we need for reading the Bible well. We need to read the Bible in light of Christ. Not only does all the fullness of the Godhead dwell in Jesus (Col. 1:19), but the whole story of the Bible finds its focus in Him. The apostles claimed that all the promises of God find their "Yes" in Christ (2 Cor. 1:20). This means that we need to read the Bible understanding that everything in the whole story relates to Christ in some way; He is at the center of the story.

The apostle Paul understood this truth. He often connected his proclamation of the Messiah to the words that Moses and the prophets wrote down. His assumption was that the Old Testament was predicting the life and ministry of Jesus. Look at his testimony before King Agrippa in Acts 26:22-23:

> 22 To this very day, I have obtained help that comes from God, and
> I stand and testify to both small and great, saying nothing else
> than what the prophets and Moses said would take place— 23 that
> the Messiah must suffer, and that as the first to rise from the dead,
> He would proclaim light to our people and to the Gentiles.
> **ACTS 26:22-23**

As Paul noted here, many passages in the Old Testament prophesied about Jesus and key events in His life, ministry, death, and resurrection. These form the backbone of the Bible's story and provide key reference points for us to understand the significance of the parts and the fuller message of the whole.

Paul was under the firm conviction that his Scriptures, what we call the Old Testament, spoke clearly about Christ in His suffering, His resurrection, and His message of salvation to both Jews and Gentiles. Christ is "the stone that the builders rejected" (Ps. 118:22). Christ is the One who "bore our sicknesses, and He carried our pains; but we in turn regarded Him stricken, struck down by God, and afflicted. But He was pierced because of our transgressions, crushed because of our iniquities; punishment for our peace was on Him, and we are healed by His wounds" (Isa. 53:4-5).

Christ is the exalted Lord to whom every knee will bow (Ps. 110:1; cf. Isa. 45:23; Rom. 14:10; Phil. 2:9-11). Paul's conviction about the Christ-centered nature of God's Word goes back to Christ Himself, who read the Scriptures in light of Himself. Speaking to the religious teachers of His day, Jesus said, "You pore over the Scriptures because you think you have eternal life in them, yet they testify about Me" (John 5:39).

After the resurrection, as Jesus talked to the two disciples on the road to Emmaus, He pointed them to this way of reading the Scriptures: "Then beginning with Moses and all the Prophets, He interpreted for them the things concerning Himself in all the Scriptures" (Luke 24:27).

A Christological reading of the Bible does not mean that every passage in Scripture speaks about Christ specifically. But it does mean that every passage relates to the message and person of Christ in some way.

> Why is it important to read the whole Bible in light of Jesus' work?

> What happens when our Bible reading is disconnected from Jesus' work for us?

As light is shown on Jesus, as we know more of Him in the fullness of what Scripture reveals about Him, that revelation casts large shadows over the whole of the Bible. As we grow to understand more of Christ, we will grow in our understanding of the entire story of the Bible. As we grow in our knowledge of the whole story of the Bible, we will grow in a fuller understanding of Christ.

> For you, is the Bible more a jumble of fragmented stories, psalms, proverbs, and teachings, or is it a unified whole? Why?

> In the past, what has helped you grasp the whole story of Scripture? How might we grow in reading the whole story in light of Christ?

3 Read the Bible in Community

There is a third "lens" that we need in order to read the Bible well—the lens of community.

Christian community is one of the greatest gifts we have as believers, and the ability to gather together around God's Word is a special aspect of that gift. Sometimes we think of Bible reading as if we were simply individuals in isolation studying words on a page. This may be one aspect of reading the Bible, but Scripture shows us that God's Word belongs to us before it belongs to me. We are to read this book together. Watch how Paul, in Colossians 3:16-17, connected God's Word to our community gatherings:

> 16 Let the message about the Messiah dwell richly among you, teaching
> and admonishing one another in all wisdom, and singing psalms,
> hymns, and spiritual songs, with gratitude in your hearts to God.
> 17 And whatever you do, in word or in deed, do everything in the name
> of the Lord Jesus, giving thanks to God the Father through Him.
> **COLOSSIANS 3:16-17**

What does it mean for us to "let the message about the Messiah dwell richly among" us? As we saw in the previous point, all of the Scriptures bear witness to Christ, the Messiah; so the message of the Scriptures, what we know as both the Old and New Testaments, should fill our lives and conversations.

The main verb in this passage is an exhortation translated "Let...dwell." The term translated as "richly" (*plousiōs*) refers to something that is abundant and is related to other Greek words in the New Testament that have to do with wealth or having plenty of something. Paul said that the message about Jesus should dwell among us, or be right at home in our interactions with each other. In other words, we should talk a lot about that message as central to what we do when we meet together as a community of faith.

Further, the Word dwelling among us provides the basis for us "teaching and admonishing one another in all wisdom." How can we grow in knowing the message of the Bible? One way is to teach and be taught in community. And as teaching takes place, it is natural for "admonishing" to take place. The term rendered as "admonishing" has to do with counseling someone, especially in a way that warns them concerning improper behavior.

So, as we live in community with one another, allowing the Word to thrive among us, we learn, but we also have the grace and responsibility to help each other live out Christ's message effectively. Of course, this has to be done "in all wisdom" and in a context of offering worship and thanks to God.

When was the last time someone graciously admonished you and challenged you in your spiritual walk?

A truly Word-oriented community walks worthy of the gospel (Phil. 1:27) and is constantly drawn to worship God. As we read the Bible the way it should be read, we need each other. We need the multiple voices around the room. We need perspective. We need admonition. We need the multi-voice "choir" that leads us to God's throne on a consistent basis. We need the Word to "dwell richly" among us so we can encourage one another to go on living for Christ and advancing His cause in the world. We were never meant to read the Bible nor attempt to live the Christian life in isolation from our brothers and sisters in Christ.

It is the community's orientation to the Word that gives us the support we need. A community strong in the Word can provide the perspective, encouragement, and strength needed to stand up in the face of anything that comes our way.

This is the way of Christian community. Thus, the community can help us read the Word better; the community can help us read the Word more consistently; and the community can help us read the Word with integrity. We need each other and find strength in each other.

Make a list of ways you interact with the Bible in the context of your local church.

What might be some dangers of studying the Bible apart from other believers?

GROUP STUDY

Warm Up

This week's individual study focused on the different lenses through which we read the Scriptures. As a group, think about why reading the Bible through these lenses is so important and discuss the following questions:

In our personal communication, why do we consider it unfair to take someone's words "out of context"?

When have you experienced negative consequences of someone taking your words out of context?

What are some dangers of taking Scripture out of context?

We are to read the Bible in light of the Bible, which means we shouldn't isolate one text from the rest of Scripture. We are also to read the Bible as one great story that points us to Jesus Christ. Finally, we are to read the Bible in community with other believers so we can be strengthened for the mission God has given us. As we grow in our ability to read the Bible in these ways, we grow in a more effective understanding of Scripture.

Discussion

During this time you will have an opportunity to discuss what God revealed to you during the week. Listed below are some of the questions from your daily reading assignments. They will guide your small-group discussion.

1. What are some tools we might use to help ourselves and others read the Bible in light of the Bible?

2. Why is it important to read the whole Bible in light of Jesus' work?

3. What happens when our Bible reading is disconnected from Jesus' work for us?

4. When did you begin to see the Bible as a unified whole instead of a disjointed collection of individual stories?

5. In the past, what has helped you grasp the whole story of Scripture? How might we grow in reading the whole story in light of Christ?

6. When was the last time someone graciously admonished you and challenged you in your spiritual walk?

7. Make a list of ways you interact with the Bible in the context of your local church. What place does God's Word have within your Christian community?

8. What might be some dangers of studying the Bible apart from other believers?

Conclusion

Years ago, a professor from a Christian college was attending a conference in a large city. To save money, he roomed at the conference hotel with a colleague from another university. Having an especially early breakfast meeting one morning, he arose before sunrise to shower and dress for the day. Not wanting to disturb his roommate, he reached for his glasses on the nightstand and made his way to the bathroom in the dark. Suddenly, the scant light filtering through the curtains in the room looked odd; his vision was blurry. He was momentarily disoriented, but he continued on to the bathroom.

After showering and getting dressed in the dark, he again felt a bit dizzy and disoriented, briefly wondering if he were getting sick or had some terrible condition manifesting itself. As he left the room and walked down the hall, his vision began to blur again. Yet all became clear as he walked up to the mirrored doors of the elevator that would take him to the hotel lobby. As he looked at his reflection in the mirror, he noticed that his glasses had changed color!

Inadvertently, in the dark, he had picked up his roommate's glasses, which were the same size and style as his but were a different color and a different prescription. Putting on the wrong glasses made the world go blurry.

As we grow in our ability to read the Bible in these ways, we grow into hearing the message of Scripture more effectively and, hopefully, living the Scripture more consistently. Having the right lenses in place will help keep the Bible in better focus, and the Bible in turn will give greater clarity to all aspects of our lives.

Spend some time praying this for yourself and for your group:

> "God, thank you for Your Son and the salvation You provided through Him. Thank you for Your perfect plan that You have revealed to us in Scripture. We desire to magnify Jesus in our lives. Lead us to a clear understanding as we read Your Word. And as we walk in faith, illuminate with wisdom the paths You've set before us. May Jesus be the center of our lives. Amen."

1. Mark L. Strauss, *How to Read the Bible in Changing Times* (Grand Rapids: Baker, 2011), 56.
2. Dietrich Bonhoeffer, *Life Together* (New York: HarperOne, 1954), 54.

Only in the Holy Scriptures do we learn to know our own history. The God of Abraham, Isaac, and Jacob is the God and Father of Jesus Christ and our Father. [2]

DIETRICH BONHOEFFER

NOTES

_____

_____

_____

_____

_____

_____

_____

_____

_____

_____

_____

_____

_____

THE GOSPEL PROJECT

Session 3

Paying Attention to Context

A text without a context becomes a pretext for a proof text.[1]

D. A. CARSON

INDIVIDUAL STUDY

When we read or study the Bible, there is no more basic principle for interpretation than understanding the context of the passage. Context is vitally important for two main reasons.

First, human language works on the basis of various types of context. In fact, we could say that words have no specific meaning apart from context. Read the following illustration that demonstrates how vital context is for understanding human communication. What is being described in this brief paragraph?

Seashore is a better place than the street. At first, it is better to run than to walk. You may have to try several times. It takes some skill, but it is easy to learn. Even young children can enjoy it. Birds seldom get too close. Rain, however, soaks in very fast. One needs lots of room. If there are no complications, it can be very peaceful. A rock will serve as an anchor.

> Why is this paragraph incomprehensible apart from context? What kind of context is needed to make sense of the author's intent?

Now read it again. But this time with just one bit of context: the word *kite*. Notice how much difference that one word makes in your reading of the paragraph.

The second reason we need to study context is that God has chosen to communicate His Word to us in human language. Specifically, God has chosen particular places, times, cultures, and ways to communicate biblical truth. Words and stories, narratives and metaphors—these carry powerful meaning to every individual. This is how the human race communicates and understands each other. So when God communicates with us, it is important to seek to understand His Word in the various contexts in which He gave it.

We want to learn to read the Bible carefully—being aware of the various contexts in which the words were communicated. In this session, we will examine three areas of context (literary, historical, and theological) and why they are important as we seek to apply the Bible to our lives today.

Throughout the week engage these daily study sections on your own. Each of these examines a different aspect of reading the Bible within the proper context. There are three daily readings to prepare you before your group meets for this session. Interact with the Scriptures, and be ready to interact with your small group.

Understand the Literary Context

When we talk about "taking a passage out of context," we normally are referring to *literary context*. Years ago, in a rather striking example of abusing literary context, a church bulletin proudly displayed the church's theme passage across the top: "All these things will I give thee, if thou wilt fall down and worship me" (Matt 4:9, KJV). Of course, in its original context, the statement was on the lips of the Devil as he tempted Jesus to turn His back on the Father! This is not a fitting theme verse for a church.

But we too may be so used to reading certain passages a particular way that we neglect literary context without even knowing it. John 2:1-12 speaks of Jesus' first miracle, the changing of water into wine at the wedding feast in Cana. We're going to keep coming back to this passage as we seek to understand its various contexts.

> [1] On the third day a wedding took place in Cana of Galilee. Jesus' mother was there, and [2] Jesus and His disciples were invited to the wedding as well. [3] When the wine ran out, Jesus' mother told Him, "They don't have any wine." [4] "What has this concern of yours to do with Me, woman?" Jesus asked. "My hour has not yet come." [5] "Do whatever He tells you," His mother told the servants. [6] Now six stone water jars had been set there for Jewish purification. Each contained 20 or 30 gallons. [7] "Fill the jars with water," Jesus told them. So they filled them to the brim. [8] Then He said to them, "Now draw some out and take it to the chief servant." And they did. [9] When the chief servant tasted the water (after it had become wine), he did not know where it came from—though the servants who had drawn the water knew. He called the groom [10] and told him, "Everyone sets out the fine wine first, then, after people have drunk freely, the inferior. But you have kept the fine wine until now." [11] Jesus performed this first sign in Cana of Galilee. He displayed His glory, and His disciples believed in Him. [12] After this, He went down to Capernaum, together with His mother, His brothers, and His disciples, and they stayed there only a few days.
>
> JOHN 2:1-12

Notice the cryptic little statement "My hour has not yet come." How should we understand this statement? We need to consider the broader literary context because this statement is repeated several times in the Gospel of John. Consider the following passages:

- "Then they tried to seize Him. Yet no one laid a hand on Him because His hour had not yet come" (7:30).
- "He spoke these words by the treasury, while teaching in the temple complex. But no one seized Him, because His hour had not come" (8:20). But later, in John 12:23 and 13:1, Jesus says that His hour has come:
- "Jesus replied to them, 'The hour has come for the Son of Man to be glorified'" (12:23; cf. 12:27).
- "Before the Passover Festival, Jesus knew that His hour had come to depart from this world to the Father. Having loved His own who were in the world, He loved them to the end" (13:1).

By looking at the broader literary context of the Gospel, we learn that in speaking of "the hour," Jesus referred to the time of His death and resurrection—the final week of His ministry. Beginning with His cryptic statement in chapter 2, the whole first half of John's Gospel builds to a climactic point that focuses on that most important of weeks. The statement in 2:4 whets our appetites and arouses our curiosity as readers, making us wonder what He is talking about. But we have to keep reading to find out. This insight is the beginning of an answer to what is going on when Jesus said, "My hour has not yet come." To consider other dimensions of Jesus' statement, we need to consider other aspects of context.

What passages of Scripture have you misinterpreted because you did not understand the literary context?

2 Understand the Historical Context

Historical context "has to do with historical events in the biblical era, either events recorded in the pages of Scripture or events that form the backdrop for the biblical story."[2] Sometimes works of literature have a historical framework built into them. For instance, if you are reading a biography or a work of history, paying close attention to the sequence of events is very important, and understanding the broader history of the time described can help in understanding those specific events.

What are some examples of famous literature that need to be interpreted within a certain historical and cultural context in order to make sense?

When dealing with events in the biblical narratives, we need to begin with the most basic events surrounding a particular story and ask the significance of those events and their sequence. So in dealing with Jesus' miracle of turning water into wine in John 2, we need to ask when this miracle happened in the broader story and what hints concerning the time frame John included.

For instance, it is significant that, as for immediate historical context, John has been counting "days" ever since John 1:19. In 2:1 we are told that this wedding took place "on the third day," but in the total reckoning of days, beginning at 1:19, D. A. Carson points out that this is the seventh day since John started counting. He further notes that this seventh day echoes the seven days of creation in Genesis 1.[3]

So, paying attention to the immediate historical context offered us by John leads to a theological insight. It is significant that here at the beginning of Jesus' ministry (again, this is historical context), we are offered a picture of Jesus' ministry as "creative" in a way that points to creation, the beginning of the world. In a sense, Jesus' ministry has a great deal to do with "re-creation" (think of the "new birth" in John 3).

As we saw when dealing with literary context, Jesus' "hour" is mentioned here at the beginning of His ministry, and that "hour" is explained at the end of His ministry. This framing of the events in Jesus' ministry forms another aspect of the historical context of our passage. (In narrative, literary and historical context at times overlap.) In short, the "history" of Jesus' ministry is framed by these references to "the hour" of His death and exaltation, underscoring the centrality of those events.

How does understanding the historical context of a movie or book give you insight into the work's significance?

What happens when you interpret something apart from its history?

Another dimension of historical context has to do with the *cultural context* of a particular time in history. "Culture" has to do with a number of things—attitudes, perspectives, patterns of behavior, and ways of speaking in a particular society. Such dynamics are vitally important for an accurate reading of the Bible.

For instance, in discussing John 2 in *Read the Bible for Life*, Andreas Köstenberger spoke of wedding feasts in the first century:

> *"A wedding often was a week-long ceremony, and the family was responsible for hosting their guests for the whole week. Running out of wine would have been very embarrassing socially, reflecting negatively on the family's ability to celebrate the bride and groom properly. It would be like a family today failing to provide food and drinks at a wedding reception. Those attending would be embarrassed for the family. So essentially what Mary was asking Jesus to do was to preserve the honor of that family, in whom she seems to have had some vested interest. In that culture honor and shame were very important concepts, much more important than in our culture."* [4]

So, from a cultural standpoint, we learn more about Mary's motivation for bringing this request to Jesus. She probably did not want the family to be embarrassed at the lack of wine. At the same time, Jesus used Mary's request to do something that displayed His glory, or shined a light on His identity, as we will see in the next point. Thus, the historical and cultural elements of the story of the miracle at Cana help us grasp various dimensions of the story.

3 Understand the Theological Context

A third aspect of context has to do with the *theological context* of a passage. We can define theological context as "how a passage fits in the tapestry of the Bible as a whole." In other words, how does a passage you are studying or reading contribute to or play off of broader themes or theological ideas communicated in the Bible?

For instance, 1 Peter 2:4-5 reads, "Coming to Him, a living stone—rejected by men but chosen and valuable to God—you yourselves, as living stones, are being built into a spiritual house for a holy priesthood to offer spiritual sacrifices acceptable to God through Jesus Christ."

If you were to take into consideration other parts of Scripture, what would you say Peter meant when he wrote that believers in Christ are "living stones"?

One popular Bible teacher, commenting on this passage, points to the stone (it is the same word in Greek) in front of Jesus' tomb, explaining that being "living stones" means that we move out of the way so light can be shined on the resurrection of Jesus. But besides the fact that the word for "stone" is used literally in the Gospel account and figuratively in 1 Peter 2, this interpretation misses a very important theological context of the passage.

In the Old Testament, the temple was celebrated as the dwelling place of God. But under the new covenant, believers have become the new dwelling place of God, the new temple (1 Cor. 3:16; 6:19). Now, instead of having to travel to the city of Jerusalem to experience the presence of God, people can encounter God's presence through the "living stones," the "spiritual house" comprised of God's people throughout the world! Understanding the broader theological context of the concept of "temple" in the Bible can help us in understanding 1 Peter 2:4-5.

What's the difference between these two interpretations?

How could these different approaches lead you down two different paths of listening to God?

Similarly, there is also a very important theological context behind the wedding at Cana in John 2:1-12. If you remember from our discussion thus far, Mary wanted Jesus to do something about the wine crisis at the wedding. She came to Jesus with a practical need. But Jesus used the moment to point to a bigger theological issue—His own identity, what His ability to do such a miracle says about who He is and what He came to do.

The prophets of the Old Testament described the time of the coming Messiah as an age when wine would flow abundantly (Jer. 31:10-14; Hos. 14; Amos 9:8-15). In His teaching, Jesus took up a wedding feast as a symbol of the culmination of the messianic age (Matt. 22:1-14; 25:1-13). So, in turning the water into wine at the wedding in Cana, Jesus was doing much more than merely meeting the need of the moment—He was acting out His identity and the role for which the Father sent Him into the world. He is the Messiah of whom the prophets foretold.[5]

What are other theological themes in Scripture that are important for understanding individual passages of Scripture?

GROUP STUDY

Warm Up

Context refers to the circumstances that form the setting for a passage of Scripture. When we make an effort to discover the context for a passage of Scripture, we find important clues for better understanding the meaning of that passage. In this session, we examined three areas of context (literary, historical, and theological) and why they are important as we seek to apply the Bible to our lives today.

> **Which of these three areas of context do you find easiest to incorporate into your personal Bible study?**

> **In dealing with all three aspects of context—literary, historical-cultural, and theological—what are some tools that can help us stay on track?**

As a group, consider the following tools to help make sense of the contexts of Scripture:

First, if you don't have a good study Bible, such as the *HCSB Study Bible*, you need to get one. Among other things, a good study Bible includes rich notes at the bottom of the page that help you understand a passage. These notes often include insights on broader issues of context.

Second, a good Bible dictionary, such as the *Holman Illustrated Bible Dictionary*, offers outlines of books that can help you discern a passage's literary context and entries for learning more about historical and cultural contexts. Such a dictionary will also offer articles on important theological themes of the Bible, which can be invaluable in studying theological context.

Third, a good commentary on the book of the Bible you are studying can be invaluable.

Discussion

During this time you will have an opportunity to discuss what God revealed to you during the week. Listed below are some of the questions from your daily reading assignments. They will guide your small-group discussion.

1. What passages of Scripture have you misinterpreted because you did not understand the literary context?

2. What are some examples of famous literature that need to be interpreted within a certain historical and cultural context in order to make sense?

3. How does understanding the historical context of a movie or book give you insight into the work's significance?

4. What happens when you interpret something apart from its history?

5. What are other theological themes in Scripture that are important for understanding individual passages of Scripture?

Conclusion

We might conclude by reflecting on how our own context also shapes the way we read. In *What Do They Hear?*, scholar Mark Allen Powell tells of the various reactions of his students to the parable of the prodigal son, noting that his American, Russian, and Tanzanian students hear the parable in very different ways.

One-hundred percent of the American students heard the part about the son squandering his money. Only 6 percent of them emphasized the fact that there was a famine. Among the Russian students, 34 percent mentioned the squandering of the son's resources, while 84 percent heard the part about the famine. The Tanzanian students saw a major issue in the lack of help the son received from foreigners, suggesting that those in the foreign land should have helped the "immigrant," and they saw the father's house as primarily symbolic of the kingdom where the young man was taken care of.[6]

Powell's experience with his students emphasizes well that we hear the Bible out of our own cultural contexts, and we need to be aware of those contexts. But the foundation must be laid by tuning in, as much as possible, to the literary, historical, and theological contexts of any given passage. For instance, as we read the parable of the prodigal, do we grasp the importance of the broader literary context of the chapter in which Luke set the tone for all three parables about lost things (Luke 15:1-2)? In terms of historical-cultural background, do we understand the significance of the father in the story running? Or the son feeding pigs? Do we grasp the big, theological theme of God as a Father who loves His wayward children? Learning more about such issues of context can push back and correct our natural tendencies to shape the biblical text in the image of our own cultures. Such a foundation is vital for understanding and living the Bible appropriately.

Spend some time praying this for yourself and for your group:

"God, continue to teach us how to better listen as You speak through Your Word. Help us rise above what is culturally shallow, and give us the intellectual and spiritual fortitude to interpret Your Words in the proper context. We want to hear You so we can obey and glorify You. Amen."

1. D. A. Carson, "One Way (Matthew 7:13-27)," in *Only One Way?* ed. Richard Phillips (Wheaton: Crossway, 2006), 134.
2. Andreas Köstenberger, quoted in *Read the Bible for Life*, by George H. Guthrie (Nashville: B&H, 2011), 39.
3. D. A. Carson, *The Gospel According to John*, in *The Pillar New Testament Commentary* (Grand Rapids: Eerdmans, 1991), 168.
4. Andreas Köstenberger, quoted in *Read the Bible for Life*, by George H. Guthrie, 37-38.
5. D. A. Carson, *The Gospel According to John*, in *The Pillar New Testament Commentary*, 172.
6. Mark Allen Powell, *What Do They Hear?* (Nashville: Abingdon, 2007), 16-17,26-27.
7. Nicholas Perrin, "Foreword," in *From Abraham to Paul*, by Andrew E. Steinmann (St. Louis: Concordia, 2011), xxiv.

> We should be grateful, because God made history and history matters...[W]hen we are fully persuaded that sacred history meshes with the history in which we live and move and have our being, that is when biblical faith becomes a real possibility. [7]
>
> **NICHOLAS PERRIN**

NOTES

THE
GOSPEL
PROJECT

Session 4

Understanding Old Testament Genres

Genre identification can make or break the proper
interpretation of a biblical book or passage. [1]

MARK STRAUSS

INDIVIDUAL STUDY

When we speak about context, we must consider the *genre* of a particular book or passage. A science textbook presents a specific kind of writing; a piece of historical fiction uses another. Both of these types of writing have "rules" that govern how we "interpret" them. Authors write various kinds of literature or publications assuming that their readers will know how to read the particular piece of writing in line with the author's intentions.

No one expects a political cartoon to be historically accurate. No one expects poetry to be scientifically descriptive. We don't read a comic strip the same way we read a biography. We don't read a history book the same way we read a political cartoon.

> Consider a few examples of different kinds of writing in our culture—essays, news articles, opinion, fiction, children's books, and biography. What are the purposes of these kinds of writing?

The Bible contains various kinds of literature, including narrative, poetry, law, prophecy, proverbs, Gospels, letters, and a form of writing called apocalyptic. Bob Stein, in his book *A Basic Guide to Interpreting the Bible: Playing by the Rules*, points out that each type of literature in the Bible has its own "rules" that govern how we should read it, drawing a comparison between such rules and the rules of a game.[2] For instance, no one would sit down and try to play backgammon or chess without having a basic grasp of how the game is played. The result would be immediate defeat.

And yet, we often attempt to read the various kinds of literature found in the Bible without any orientation to the rules of how a person in the ancient world would hear and understand these types of literature.

In this session and the next, we will take a look at basic guidelines for reading various genres found in the Bible. Here we will consider four prominent types of literature found in the Old Testament: narrative, law, poetry, and wisdom. With each we will consider important "rules of the game" for how they can be read appropriately.

Throughout the week engage these daily study sections on your own. Each of these examines the different aspects of reading the Old Testament. There are three daily readings to prepare you before your group meets for this session. Interact with the Scriptures, and be ready to interact with your group.

1 Interpreting Old Testament Narrative

On one level, the stories we find in the Bible constitute a type of literature that is easiest for us to grasp. We all love a good story. And stories are very important to our lives.

A little less than half of the Old Testament is in story form, so we need to take time to think through how to read these stories well. Let's talk through several guidelines or rules for reading Old Testament narrative as we look at Exodus 2:1-10, which recounts the birth of Moses.

> [1] Now a man from the family of Levi married a Levite woman. [2] The woman became pregnant and gave birth to a son; when she saw that he was beautiful, she hid him for three months. [3] But when she could no longer hide him, she got a papyrus basket for him and coated it with asphalt and pitch. She placed the child in it and set it among the reeds by the bank of the Nile. [4] Then his sister stood at a distance in order to see what would happen to him.
> [5] Pharaoh's daughter went down to bathe at the Nile while her servant girls walked along the riverbank. Seeing the basket among the reeds, she sent her slave girl to get it. [6] When she opened it, she saw the child—a little boy, crying. She felt sorry for him and said, "This is one of the Hebrew boys."
> [7] Then his sister said to Pharaoh's daughter, "Should I go and call a woman from the Hebrews to nurse the boy for you?"
> [8] "Go," Pharaoh's daughter told her. So the girl went and called the boy's mother. [9] Then Pharaoh's daughter said to her, "Take this child and nurse him for me, and I will pay your wages." So the woman took the boy and nursed him. [10] When the child grew older, she brought him to Pharaoh's daughter, and he became her son. She named him Moses, "Because," she said, "I drew him out of the water."
> EXODUS 2:1-10

1. The first question we should ask of Old Testament narrative is this: How is God the ultimate hero of this Old Testament story?

To follow up, we should ask:

- How is God working things out in this story?
- What does this story tell me about God and what God values?
- How does this story fit into God's bigger plan?
- How does covenant with God fit in?

It is interesting that our immediate passage does not even mention God. So where should we look to see God's part in this story? We need to look in the broader context. How does God's role in Exodus 1 lay the foundation for the story of the birth of Moses? (For an answer to the question of how this story relates to God's covenant, see Ex. 2:24-25.)

2. We also should ask key literary questions about this story.

Spend a few moments answering the following questions about the story we just read:

- Who are the main characters of the story, and what is the setting?
- What is the nature of the tension in the story? What are key turning points?
- What seems to be the main point of the story? (Notice especially how the author begins and ends the story.)
- How does this story contribute to the Bible's grand narrative?

3. Finally, we should ask how the lives of the characters in the story parallel our lives today or how they should influence us.

- Are the people in the story serving as positive or negative examples?
- What are the differences between us and them? Similarities?

In some ways Moses' story is very unique. He would be raised up as a unique deliverer in the history of Israel. Still, we can learn from the story of Moses. Hebrews 11:23 celebrates the faith of Moses' parents. Moses himself was not perfect, as seen in his murder of the Egyptian in Exodus 2:12. Yet, even this should give us encouragement that God uses very broken and imperfect people in His great plan.

How did these guidelines help you understand Moses' story better?

2 Interpreting the Law

One of the more difficult areas to read and interpret for the modern Christian is the Old Testament law. Many of the laws just seem so foreign—and they are!

Mark Strauss highlights this fact by pointing to a spoof letter that has floated around the Internet. In the letter, the writer, provocatively taking the Bible very literally, asks a talk show host for advice:

- When I burn a bull on the altar as a sacrifice, I know it creates a pleasing odor for the Lord (Lev. 1:9). The problem is my neighbors. They claim the odor is not pleasing to them. How should I deal with this?
- I would like to sell my daughter into slavery, as it suggests in Exodus 21:7. In this day and age, what do you think would be a fair price for her?
- Leviticus 25:44 states that I may buy slaves from the nations that are around us. A friend of mine claims that this applies to Mexicans but not to Canadians. Can you clarify?
- I have a neighbor who insists on working on the Sabbath. Exodus 35:2 clearly states he should be put to death. Am I morally obligated to kill him myself?
- Leviticus 21:20 states that I may not approach the altar of God if I have a defect in my sight. I have to admit that I wear reading glasses. Does my vision have to be 20/20 or is there some wiggle room here?[3]

What are some parts of the Old Testament law that trouble you?

How would you respond to someone who attempts to discredit the Bible by pointing out obscure, seemingly irrelevant rules?

The original author of this spoof list of questions was arguing against biblical authority, attempting to show how absurd it is to try to live according to the Bible. But the spoof misses very important guidelines that should guide modern Christians, who are no longer under the old covenant law, in how they read and consider these laws today. What are those guidelines?

1. Affirm that the laws are part of God's Word to us.
2. Determine how the laws relate to the broader story in which they are found.
3. Read the laws in light of their cultural context.
4. Recognize that the laws are often not applicable to us in the same way they were applicable to the people under the old covenant, but they are still applicable to us in important ways.
5. Discern if the New Testament has any further comment on a law.

As a simple exercise, let's take this one verse from the Old Testament (Deut. 19:14) and apply the guidelines listed above.

> ¹⁴ You must not move your neighbor's boundary marker,
> established at the start in the inheritance you will receive in
> the land the LORD your God is giving you to possess.
> **DEUTERONOMY 19:14**

First, let's affirm that this is God's revelation to us and therefore is profitable for us. *Second*, the law actually has a very important place in the broader story, one quite overt in the passage itself. With the Israelites moving into the promised land, a land that would be subdivided among the people, family boundaries would be very important. *Third*, how would this relate to the cultural context of the time? The *Zondervan Illustrated Bible Backgrounds Commentary on the Old Testament* tells us that stones were often used to mark property boundaries, and moving such stones incurred heavy penalties in most cultures of the ancient Near East.[4] So this law of Israel was in line with a broader understanding of ethics at the time. *Fourth*, we can discern a principle behind this law and God's putting it into the law of Israel, for basic to this law was an understanding of human rights. People had a right to their own property and that right should not be violated. *Fifth*, although the New Testament neither reiterates nor suggests that Deuteronomy 19:14 has been done away with, God's laws have been written on the hearts of the new covenant people (Heb. 8:10). Motivated by the Holy Spirit, we should be the first in our own culture to stand up for the property rights of others and the first to practice restitution when we have somehow damaged another's property.

What would be ways that we might fulfill the principle behind this law today? How might we show respect for the property of our neighbors?

Interpreting Poetry & Wisdom Literature

Two other types of literature in the Old Testament are wisdom literature and poetry. We will focus on the two most familiar examples of these genres, proverbs and psalms, respectively.

Wisdom Literature. When we speak of wisdom literature, we simply mean literature that seeks to help a person live wisely for God or think through the perplexities of human life. Job, parts of Psalms, Proverbs, Ecclesiastes, and Song of Songs are all considered wisdom literature (large parts of these certainly are poetic as well). Consider the following guidelines when reading wisdom literature:

1. At its most basic level, wisdom literature offers general guidelines for how life is best lived.

Proverbs, for instance, are not promises and should not be read as such. For example, Proverbs 9:11 says, "For by Wisdom your days will be many, and years will be added to your life." Does this proverb mean that wise people never die young? Is this a promise of long life for the wise? No. The proverb simply means that, as a general rule, a wise person is more likely to live a long life than a fool. Fools end up hurting themselves and even shortening their lives.

2. Many of the proverbs offer universal truths that are immediately applicable in the modern world, but elements of some proverbs need further study.

Proverbs 21:20 says, "Precious treasure and oil are in the dwelling of a wise person, but a foolish man consumes them." Most of us do not keep "precious treasure" at home, and most of us have various forms of oil at home. Are we to understand that it is "wise" to keep precious treasure at home? No, the point of this proverb is that wisdom often leads to a life that prospers. A fool consumes all his resources on his appetites. A wise person saves.

At the same time, many of us have olive oil at home, yet the passage is not saying that we shouldn't consume the oil we often use in cooking. Rather, a bit of study would show us that the oil of which the proverb speaks was one of the most important and useful resources a person could have—being used for cooking, lighting, medicine, and personal hygiene. In other words, the proverb celebrates a person who knows how to handle his or her resources well.

What would be a way we could live out Proverbs 21:20?

3. Those parts of wisdom literature that reflect on the perplexities of life should be read in light of the broader revelation of Scripture.

Reading a book like Job or Ecclesiastes takes a bit more skill on the part of the reader because these books are grappling with heavy questions of life, such as "Why do the righteous suffer?" and "Why does even productive life at times feel meaningless?" Again, we need to understand these books in light of their original contexts and, at the same time, read them in the broader light of Scripture.

Poetry. Let's conclude by thinking briefly about poetic literature in the Old Testament, the most popular expression of which is the psalms. We identify very easily with the psalms since they express a full range of human emotions, from the heights of joy to the depths of despair. So how might we read the psalms more effectively? Here are some guidelines for reading biblical poetry:

1. Understand that there are different kinds of psalms.

For instance, some psalms, such as Psalm 100, are psalms of praise meant to celebrate the character of God. Other psalms focus on thanksgiving or call out to God for help, while still others, such as Psalm 106, are historical psalms recounting an aspect of Israel's history. There also are psalms of lament, which give voice to grief, and messianic psalms, such as Psalm 110, that tell of the coming of Jesus.

2. Tune in to the emotion expressed in the psalm as well as the way the psalm uses figurative language.

As you note the expressions of emotion in the psalm, think through how those emotions parallel your life. Use the psalm to prompt you to praise God or to remember what He has done or to cry out to Him with specific petitions.

GROUP STUDY

Warm Up

Harold Goddard wrote, "The destiny of the world is determined less by the battles that are lost and won than by the stories it loves and believes in."[5] Various kinds of literature have a profound influence on how we think and live—driving people to do the things they do. The Old Testament begins God's story with humanity, and we are all a part of it.

Some believers find the Old Testament intimidating, but God has spoken in every era of biblical history. When we interpret the different kinds of Old Testament literature, we learn about God's activity, character, and redemptive purposes. We are also equipped to apply the Bible properly to our lives today. In this session, we learned principles for interpreting four kinds of literature: narrative, law, poetry, and wisdom.

Which of these types of literature are easiest for you to read and understand—Old Testament narrative, law, poetry, or wisdom literature? Which seem the most foreign? Why?

How should we respond to people who claim Christians just pick and choose which parts of the Bible they want to apply?

If you were explaining to a person from a very different culture than our own how to understand historical fiction or a comic strip, what would you say? What are their "rules of interpretation"?

Discussion

During this time you will have an opportunity to discuss what God revealed to you during the week. Listed below are some of the questions from your daily reading assignments. They will guide your small-group discussion.

1. Consider a few examples of different kinds of writing in our culture—essays, news articles, opinion, fiction, children's books, and biography. What are the purposes of these kinds of writing?

2. What are some parts of the Old Testament law that trouble you?

3. How would you respond to someone who attempts to discredit the Bible by pointing out obscure, seemingly irrelevant rules?

4. How did you answer that question about Deuteronomy 19:14—what would be ways that we might fulfill the principle behind this law today? How might we show a respect for the property of our neighbors?

5. What would be a way we could live out Proverbs 21:20?

Conclusion

It is vitally important for us to learn to read these various types of literature well for at least two main reasons. First, misreading these parts of Scripture can be harmful to us. Years ago, a woman whose husband had left her claimed a particular proverb as a promise from God guaranteeing that her husband would leave his mistress and return to her. He never did, and she concluded that God had "lied" to her, failing to keep His promise. In her disillusionment, she drifted away from the Lord for years, in part because she had misunderstood how to read a proverb appropriately. Reading the parts of Scripture well matters a great deal.

Second, these parts of Scripture become more meaningful to us personally as we understand them better. To hear God speak to us through any part of Scripture can be wonderfully rewarding. Hearing the literature of the Old Testament in line with how God inspired that literature to be read can help us grow in our Christian lives. This is God's Word to us, and we need to be able to read it well.

Spend some time praying this for yourself and for your group:

> "God, thank You for revealing Yourself to us in Scripture. Help us to
> see that You are good and righteous in all that You do, and give us
> wisdom as we study Your Word. Reveal Your truth to us. Amen."

1. Mark L. Strauss, *How to Read the Bible in Changing Times* (Grand Rapids: Baker, 2011), 50.
2. Robert H. Stein, *A Basic Guide to Interpreting the Bible: Playing by the Rules* (Grand Rapids: Baker, 1994), 75-78.
3. Mark L. Strauss, *How to Read the Bible in Changing Times*, 9-10.
4. Eugene E. Carpenter, "Deuteronomy," in *Genesis, Exodus, Leviticus, Numbers, Deuteronomy*, vol. 1 in *Zondervan Illustrated Bible Backgrounds Commentary*, ed. John H. Walton (Grand Rapids: Zondervan, 2009), 487-88.
5. Harold C. Goddard, *The Meaning of Shakespeare*, vol. 2 (Chicago: University of Chicago, 1951), 208.
6. Robert L. Plummer, *40 Questions About Interpreting the Bible* (Grand Rapids: Kregel, 2010), 195.

The wise interpreter is always seeking the authorial meaning of the text and does not use extraneous details for his own sermonizing flights of fancy. [6]

ROBERT PLUMMER

NOTES

Session 5

Interpreting
New Testament
Genres

The diligent reading of the word of God with the strong
resolve to get at its meaning often begets spiritual life. [1]

CHARLES SPURGEON

INDIVIDUAL STUDY

On a sitcom, three young women engage in a conversation. The first says, "Okay, well, I did something that will either make me look like a lovable goof or a horrible monster."

The second woman responds, "I'm sure it's lovable." The third responds, "I'm gonna go with monster. What do you got?"

The first woman says, "Well, there's this lady in our office who's retiring, and they were passing around a card for us to sign … But no one told me she was in a horrible car accident over the weekend and what I was signing was not a retirement card but was actually a 'get well' card. So on the card, in the hospital, next to the woman who's clinging to life are the words, 'Hey, girl. You deserve this! And at least with you gone, no one will steal my yogurt out of the fridge! P. S. Good luck wherever you wind up.'"

Retirement cards and "get well" cards are two very different types of communication. The context of genre really matters!

> When was a time you said or communicated something out of place? How did you discover your mistake?

Genre matters because God inspired His words in particular genres so they would be read in particular ways. In this session, we now turn our attention to New Testament literature, specifically considering the narratives, the letters, and the Book of Revelation. Once again, we consider various guidelines for reading each of these kinds of literature well. Our goal here is to introduce these kinds of literature so we can begin tuning in to important differences in the ways these literatures work and "speak" to us.

Throughout the week engage these daily study sections on your own. Each of these examines the different aspects of interpreting the New Testament. There are three daily readings to prepare you before your group meets for this session. Interact with the Scriptures, and be ready to interact with your small group.

1 Interpreting New Testament Narrative

Narrative makes up about 60 percent of the New Testament and comprises the four Gospels and the Book of Acts. As we discussed in our last session, narrative feels somewhat intuitive to most of us. We have a basic sense of how stories work.

Nevertheless, there are dimensions of the New Testament stories that we need to grasp as we grow in our Bible-reading skills.

1. The four Gospels together give us a full, consistent picture of Jesus, but they approach the story differently.

First of all, we have four Gospels and the Book of Acts to consider. The first three Gospels are sometimes called "the Synoptic Gospels" (*synoptic* basically means "to see from the same perspective") because Matthew, Mark, and Luke follow the same general pattern in telling the story of Jesus. Much of their material overlaps. One characteristic they share in common is that they relate the story of Jesus as a process of discovery on the part of the disciples and the readers of the story.

The three Synoptic Gospels together offer a consistent picture of Jesus, but we have a fuller picture because there are three witnesses to the story rather than just one. They do not contradict; they complement one another.

John, on the other hand, tells the story of Jesus "from heaven down." It is clear right from the beginning of John's Gospel who Jesus is. He is the Word who created the world (John 1:3). He is "the Lamb of God who takes away the sin of the world!" (1:29). In John we have a powerful proclamation of Jesus' identity. We get glimpses of that identity early on in the Synoptic Gospels, but the approach is different.

2. Understand that each Gospel, as well as the Book of Acts, offers unique emphases.

Beyond general approaches to the story of Jesus, our five narrative books in the New Testament offer particular emphases. A basic understanding of these will help us read these narrative books better.

> If you were to recommend an unbeliever read one Gospel, which one would you choose? Why?

Sometimes in unpacking their emphases, the Gospel writers are more interested in theological insight rather than exact chronology. Take the scenes of Jesus' temptation in Matthew 4 and Luke 4. In Luke's version, the second and third temptations are switched when compared to the order in Matthew's account. Luke's version culminates with the temptation to jump from the temple. Many scholars believe that Luke switched Matthew's order because he had a special concern for the temple. It is not that Luke was confused on the order of the temptations; he merely wanted to emphasize one aspect of the story in a different way.

At other points, a Gospel writer may condense or expand parts of a story. This was common practice in the ancient world in which emphasis was placed on highlighting significant parts of a story to make a point. This does not contradict the historicity of the account; it merely shines a spotlight on an aspect of the history.

Yet all of these unique emphases of the Gospels and Acts (written by Luke; extends his Gospel's emphases but adds others, such as the mission of the church to the nations) focus on one common theme: Jesus is God's promised Messiah who is now Lord of the universe. So as we work our way through any of these narrative books, we want to ask, "What does this part of the story tell me about Jesus?"

What were some of the first things you learned about Jesus when reading the Gospels and Acts?

3. We need to continue growing in our understanding of the cultural contexts reflected in these stories.

The confession of Jesus as Messiah in Mark 8 should be read against a particular cultural backdrop—specifically, the messianic expectations in the first century. There were many different expectations about the Jewish Messiah who was to come. Some did not expect a messiah. Others thought there would be two messiahs—perhaps a royal one and a priestly one. Still others expected a royal messiah who would lead the Jewish people to victory over and expulsion of the Romans from the land of Israel (see John 6:15). This last expectation is probably the one held by the disciples, as reflected in passages such as Acts 1:6b: "Lord, are You restoring the kingdom to Israel at this time?" What no one expected was a suffering Messiah.

2 Interpreting the Letters

The New Testament also contains letters. Thirteen of these letters come from Paul (four to individuals and nine to churches), and seven were written by other authors (many consider Hebrews a "sermon" rather than a letter). So what guidelines will help us approach a letter? Let's consider two of them.

1. Understand the situation that prompted the letter.

Most of the New Testament letters were "occasional," which means that a particular occasion or situation prompted the author to write. For instance, Romans was written by Paul as a theological overview of the gospel because he was delayed in visiting the church in Rome for the first time. Galatians grew out of a serious theological crisis among the churches in Galatia, which were in danger of substituting a false gospel for the true message of Christ. First Peter was prompted in part by the church suffering from severe persecution.

In the case of Philemon, the personal letter was written around A.D. 60-61 while Paul was in prison (probably in Rome). Philemon, who lived in Colossae, had a slave named Onesimus who had run away and had stolen some of Philemon's property (Philem. 15-16,18-19). Onesimus had made his way to Rome and there he met Paul, who was in prison. Paul led the runaway slave to faith in Christ, and Onesimus proved to be a valuable companion and helper to Paul (vv. 10-17). Paul then sent Onesimus back with his letter so that Onesimus and Philemon could be reconciled and so Philemon could release Onesimus to serve Paul further (vv. 14-16,20-21).[2]

Now, as we have seen with the other literary genres of the Bible, the occasions behind the New Testament letters often are shaped by the cultural and historical context of the letter. For example, when dealing with Philemon, we would want to understand more about the nature of slavery in the first century Mediterranean world. A slave could legally be executed for running away, for instance.

How does understanding the occasion of the letter help us understand the message?

2. Seek to understand the general structure of the letter.

Today, we have a general form for letters, which tends to begin with "Dear _____," and concludes with something like "Sincerely" plus the writer's name. Similarly, ancient letters normally can be divided into three parts: an opening, the letter body, and the closing.

In the ancient world, letters often began with an opening that included a prescript and a prologue. The prescript often was crafted with a *superscriptio* (the author), plus an *adscriptio* (the addressee), and followed by a *salutatio* (normally an expression of "grace and peace" in the New Testament letters).

The body of a letter fleshed out the main topics the author wanted to discuss—perhaps information, teachings, encouragement, requests, or recommendations. Finally, a letter normally included a closing.

As previously discussed of literary context, one way of getting at the structure of a book—and letters are certainly included—is to look at an outline of the book in a study Bible or Bible dictionary. With letters, we often can see in a letter's structure the logic of the letter's development as well as key themes.

Read Paul's letter to Philemon. How might it serve as a model of how to make a skillful appeal to someone today, either in a work situation or in the context of the family?

3 Interpreting Apocalyptic Literature

There is a third type of New Testament literature that we need to consider: apocalyptic, expressed especially in the Book of Revelation. The term *apocalyptic* means "revelation" or "disclosure." In fact, the very first word of the last book of the New Testament is *apocalypsis*, which is normally translated as "the revelation." The Book of Revelation is one of the most difficult books of the Bible to interpret. This is directly related to *why* apocalyptic was used as a form of writing in the ancient world and *how* apocalyptic literature was crafted. God gave John "the disclosure" in this unique and powerful form, so we need to understand a few things about it.

1. Apocalyptic literature often was written in a context of persecution to give encouragement to those being persecuted.

Parts of the book are prophetic, speaking of God's ultimate judgment on the evil power structures of the world. The prophecies are meant to give immediate encouragement to those who are suffering injustice because of their faith in Christ.

Notice those parts of the book that speak of the "witnesses" (Rev. 2:13; 11:3; 17:6) or those under the throne who had died for Christ (20:4). Revelation was written at a time when the Roman Empire was severely persecuting believers in Asia Minor. John was given the revelation by Christ to provide strong encouragement for the believers in the churches of the area (and to us) as they faced harsh persecution for the faith.

> Since persecution is a primary backdrop for Revelation, what are specific places in the world today where the book could be especially helpful to followers of Christ?

2. The main message of the Book of Revelation is that God—not the Roman emperor—is in ultimate control of the universe.

In a church Bible study context, when asked what the Book of Revelation is about, one New Testament scholar responded simply, "God wins!"

God's work among the nations has a specific agenda. Through Christ, His followers are proclaiming God's glory by sharing the gospel among the nations. The gospel, the Messiah, and the Messiah's people are opposed by Satan and Satan's evil forces in the world. These forces are often expressed in the form of evil, abusive political systems.

Now, during the time of persecution, it looks like the evil forces are winning. But Revelation pulls back the curtain of the universe to reveal a greater reality. God sits on the throne of the universe. In fact, the word "throne" is used 37 times in the book, and the "court" of heaven is depicted as a courtroom from which God judges the world and the evil forces opposing Him. At the end of the age, God will bring His judgment to a climactic point, shutting down those evil forces.

3. The communication of this important message involves the use of graphic word pictures and symbols, many taken from the Old Testament.

The symbolism of Revelation functions to represent greater realities through a striking picture. Think, for instance, of how a political cartoon works. If you see a cartoon of a wagon-load of money with a donkey pulling on one end and an elephant pulling on the other, you understand its message because you understand the symbolism. What's the cartoonist's point? The power struggle between the two political parties revolves around money. In one glimpse, you "get the picture" and understand the message. The symbols of Revelation work similarly.

What's the biggest hindrance for you in reading and interpreting apocalyptic literature?

What are some ways we can bridge the gap between first-century culture and our application of Revelation today?

GROUP STUDY

Warm Up

In the last session, we focused on Old Testament genres. In this session we examine three different kinds of literature found in the New Testament—the Gospel stories, the letters of the apostles, and the apocalyptic imagery in Revelation. As God's people, it is important to understand His Word so that we can then apply His Word in our current context. As you and your group discuss the three New Testament genres from the lesson, consider the following questions:

Why is it important to keep the cross and resurrection central in our interpretation of the Gospels?

With which of the New Testament letters are you most familiar? Why that one?

When it feels like evil is getting the upper hand in the world, how do you handle such feelings or perceptions?

Discussion

The Gospels present themselves and are placed in the canon
in such a way that they hold together both the Old Testament's
witness and that of the other apostolic writings. On the one
hand they are the fulfillment of all the OT spoke of, while on the
other they are the fountainhead of all the epistolary literature.
In this way they serve the key role in all of Holy Scripture.[3]

JONATHAN PENNINGTON

During this time you will have an opportunity to discuss what God revealed to you during the week. Listed below are some of the questions from your daily reading assignments. They will guide your small-group discussion.

1. If you were to recommend an unbeliever read one Gospel, which one would you choose? Why?

2. What were some of the first things you learned about Jesus when reading the Gospels and Acts?

3. How does understanding the occasion of the letter help us understand the message?

4. Read Paul's letter to Philemon. How might it serve as a model of how to make a skillful appeal to someone today, either in a work situation or in the context of the family?

5. Since persecution is a primary backdrop for Revelation, what are specific places in the world today where the book could be especially helpful to followers of Christ?

6. What's the biggest hindrance for you in reading and interpreting apocalyptic literature?

7. What are some ways we can bridge the gap between first-century culture and our application of Revelation today?

Conclusion

On July 5, 2009, a 55-year-old amateur treasure hunter in England discovered a large hoard of Anglo-Saxon treasure. He made the discovery using a metal detector on a friend's farm in the village of Hammerwich in Staffordshire. There Terry Herbert uncovered 1,345 gold and silver artifacts that date back to the seventh century. Herbert split the profits from the find—over £3.2 million (more than $5 million)—50-50 with his farm-owner friend. This discovery is now called "The Staffordshire Hoard."[4]

When it was found, Terry Herbert put the treasure in 244 bags. In this session we have discussed what could be called "The New Testament Hoard." There are 260 chapters in the New Testament, which contain a far greater treasure than mere gold and silver objects.

Where would we be without the New Testament? Yet we at times need to do some digging to really understand the value of our treasure. Hopefully the principles we have seen in this session will give us the needed tools.

Spend some time praying this for yourself and for your group:

> "God, thank You for Your Words of grace and comfort. Help us to hear You through Your Word as we partner with You in sharing the gospel. Give us a love for all of Your people. Give us compassion for all of Your creation. We will cling to the real hope that, in the end, You win! Amen."

1. C. H. Spurgeon, "How to Read the Bible," The Spurgeon Archive [online], 1879 [cited 24 September 2014]. Available from the Internet: *www.spurgeon.org*.
2. Murray Harris, *Exegetical Guide to the Greek New Testament: Colossians and Philemon* (Nashville: B&H, 2010), 207.
3. Jonathan Pennington, in "The Gospel in the Gospels: A Conversation with Jonathan Pennington," by Trevin Wax, Kingdom People [online], 25 October 2012 [cited 25 September 2014]. Available from the Internet: *thegospelcoalition.org*.
4. Caroline Alexander, "Magical Mystery Treasure," *National Geographic* [online], November 2011 [cited 25 September 2014]. Available from the Internet: *ngm.nationalgeographic.com*.
5. Robert L. Plummer, *40 Questions About Interpreting the Bible* (Grand Rapids: Kregel, 2010), 279.

The letters in the New Testament are more than time-bound communication; they are works inspired by the Holy Spirit, offering authoritative instruction to the church in every age. [5]

ROBERT PLUMMER

NOTES

THE GOSPEL PROJECT

Session 6

Walking in Faithful Obedience

We must allow the Word of God to confront us, to disturb our security, to undermine our complacency and to overthrow our patterns of thought and behavior. [1]

JOHN STOTT

INDIVIDUAL STUDY

The story is told of three friends who went deer hunting together. One was a lawyer, the second a doctor, and the third a preacher. As they made their way deep into the woods, the three hunters spotted a large buck grazing in an open meadow. Simultaneously, all three hunters raised their rifles and shot. The mighty buck fell to the ground. The hunters smiled at each other, and each said, "I got 'im!" All three made their way to the meadow to inspect the deer, but as they examined the prize, they couldn't figure out whose shot had actually killed the buck.

A heated argument broke out, and a few minutes later, a game warden stopped by and asked the men what the problem was. The doctor informed the warden that they were debating who shot the buck, pointing out that all three had shot at the same time. The warden examined the deer and within a few seconds looked at the men and smiled. With an air of authoritative confidence, he announced, "It is obvious that the preacher shot the buck!" Puzzled, the hunters asked how he could tell. The officer replied, "It's easy! The bullet went in one ear and out the other."[2]

This story may be silly, but it illustrates a serious problem in many churches today. A recent survey by LifeWay Research showed that among regular church attenders, only 37 percent agreed that Bible reading and study had made a significant difference in the way they lived their lives.[3]

What gives? Perhaps the problem comes from people's perception of the function of preaching and teaching in the lives of believers. They understand sermons and Bible studies as "heard" rather than "implemented." They consider Bible reading as "something you do" rather than "something you live."

If we are not careful, we can begin to think the point of preaching, teaching, and Bible reading is merely our enjoyment of the moment rather than the transformation of our lives. The enjoyment of the moment is not a bad thing, of course, but in a biblical sense, the goal is life change.

Why do you think Christians often focus on learning God's Word while failing to obey God's Word?

Throughout the week engage these daily study sections on your own. Each of these examines the different aspects of applying and obeying God's Word. There are three daily readings to prepare you before your group meets for this session. Interact with the Scriptures, and be ready to interact with your small group.

1 Obeying God's Word

As we think about the need to obey God's Word, James 1:22-25 stands out as one of the most striking passages in the New Testament:

> 22 But be doers of the word and not hearers only, deceiving yourselves. 23 Because if anyone is a hearer of the word and not a doer, he is like a man looking at his own face in a mirror. 24 For he looks at himself, goes away, and immediately forgets what kind of man he was. 25 But the one who looks intently into the perfect law of freedom and perseveres in it, and is not a forgetful hearer but one who does good works—this person will be blessed in what he does.
>
> JAMES 1:22-25

First, notice in James 1:22 the contrast between merely "hearing" and "doing." What James described is straightforward. Hearing the Word of God is foundational but inadequate. A person could attend church year-round, listen to every sermon, take notes at every small group Bible study, and read his or her way through a "Bible in a Year" plan and still not be "biblically" engaged in the Word in the way that God desires.

Second, notice that James said a hearer who is not a doer is self-deceived. We might think of the Pharisees at this point, who were very Bible-oriented but not biblically transformed by the power of the Holy Spirit. The Pharisees had "applications" of Scripture, but these applications were legalistic "traditions of men" rather than expressions of authentic obedience to God.

What makes the difference between a legalistic tradition and an authentic application of the Word?

A person who treats God's Word in this way gives it a brief spiritual nod but doesn't seek to understand the Word by living it out. The contrast is a person who *looks intently* into the law of God and *perseveres* in it. In the ancient world, the first of these terms meant "to bend over for the purpose of looking, focused on satisfying one's curiosity." In other words, it is an "intense" or "focused" activity of concentrating on the Word. The second term, translated as "perseveres," meant to "remain" or "stay with something." So the doer stays with the Word all the way to application—"one who does good works" according to James 1:25. In other words, if you are not a doer of the Word, as James suggested, you are not okay spiritually, no matter what you think you see in the "spiritual mirror."

Persevering in doing the Word is what leads to blessing in life. The blessings of obedience are a theme deeply ingrained in the Bible from the beginning. In Deuteronomy 11:13-15 we read about those blessings as the children of Israel were about to enter the promised land: "If you carefully obey my commands I am giving you today, to love the LORD your God and worship Him with all your heart and all your soul, I will provide rain for your land in the proper time, the autumn and spring rains, and you will harvest your grain, new wine, and oil. I will provide grass in your fields for your livestock. You will eat and be satisfied." In the same way, James noted, those who persevere in obeying God's Word are blessed.

What are some of the blessings James might have been referring to?

This passage provides a powerful, foundational truth that gives a key for how the Christian life is to be lived. James often played off the teaching of his half brother, Jesus. Let the words from the following parable sink in as you think about the importance of obedience:

> 28 "But what do you think? A man had two sons. He went to the first and said, 'My son, go, work in the vineyard today.' 29 He answered, 'I don't want to!' Yet later he changed his mind and went. 30 Then the man went to the other and said the same thing. 'I will, sir,' he answered. But he didn't go. 31 Which of the two did his father's will?' " "The first," they said. Jesus said to them, "I assure you: Tax collectors and prostitutes are entering the kingdom of God before you!"
> MATTHEW 21:28-31

What are some areas of obedience in the modern church that we tend to ignore rather than carry out?

How might we change these patterns so that we are more faithful to the Word of God?

2 Living God's Word

One of the main reasons we want to give special attention to living out the Word is that obedience is a mark that we really know God. In other words, living out the truth is one way we grow in our assurance of salvation. In 1 John 2:3-6 we read:

> [3] This is how we are sure that we have come to know Him: by keeping His commands. [4] The one who says, "I have come to know Him," yet doesn't keep His commands, is a liar, and the truth is not in him. [5] But whoever keeps His word, truly in him the love of God is perfected. This is how we know we are in Him: [6] The one who says he remains in Him should walk just as He walked.
>
> 1 JOHN 2:3-6

John began by pointing out that obedience to the commands of God gives a foundation for assurance. In fact, John noted that if a person says he or she has come to know God yet does not live according to God's commands, that person is a liar. This is similar to the person who is "self-deceived" in James 1:22-25. The truth escapes the person who is not living out the Word. There is a profound disconnect between what is professed and what is expressed in action.

Why do you think John connected obedience to God's commands and our assurance of salvation?

What do our actions communicate about our beliefs?

First John highlights the spiritual disconnect between mere profession and concrete expression. If a person says he loves God yet doesn't live out His commands, something is terribly wrong spiritually. The person is lying by his words and his (lack of) actions. On the other hand, living out God's commands out of a love for God gives us great assurance. We see our relationship with God authentically manifested in our lives.

In our culture, we sense a disconnect between love and obedience. We think of love as an emotion and obedience as action. A mother may say of a horribly rebellious child, "But she really does love me," appealing to emotions rather than what is manifested in the child's life. But God has always associated love with obedience to His commands. You can't say that you love God while living contrary to His will.

What did Jesus say in John 15:10: "If you keep My commands you will remain in My love, just as I have kept My Father's commands and remain in His love." This is how our Lord Jesus lived—in perfect obedience and love for the Father. We listen to God's Word so we can walk as Christ walked (1 John 2:6). We remain in Jesus' love by keeping His commandments.

What would it look like for us to "walk as Christ walked"?

What is the significance of Christ connecting love and obedience together?

3 Applying God's Word

Whenever we move to application, we should be very specific in how we are going to live out the Word. Too often, we only get as far as "vague, idealistic gas," as C. S. Lewis called it, in our application of Scripture. What Lewis referred to were "applications" that consist of idealistic platitudes rather than concrete actions. For example, we read a passage like 1 Corinthians 13 and say, "I need to love people more." True, but this is really no application at all. Lewis pointed out that Jesus never dealt in vague idealism but rather challenged people to adjust their lives very specifically.

For instance, in Luke 6:46-49, we read these challenging words of Jesus:

> [46] "Why do you call Me 'Lord, Lord,' and don't do the things I say? [47] I will show you what someone is like who comes to Me, hears My words, and acts on them: [48] He is like a man building a house, who dug deep and laid the foundation on the rock. When the flood came, the river crashed against that house and couldn't shake it, because it was well built. [49] But the one who hears and does not act is like a man who built a house on the ground without a foundation. The river crashed against it, and immediately it collapsed. And the destruction of that house was great!"
>
> LUKE 6:46-49

Notice that Jesus' teaching emphasized action, not mere assent, and He described acting on His words as the critical foundation for a life able to withstand the storms of life. This passage comes at the end of Luke's version of the Sermon on the Mount (Luke 6:17-49; cf. Matt. 5–7). That span of teaching is full of practical, specific ways to live out Jesus' kingdom teaching. For instance, Luke 6:28-30 reads, "Bless those who curse you, pray for those who mistreat you. If anyone hits you on the cheek, offer the other also. And if anyone takes away your coat, don't hold back your shirt either. Give to everyone who asks you, and from one who takes your things, don't ask for them back."

This is anything but "vague, idealistic gas"! Jesus' expectations were very specific. What we believe is foundational, but we also need to live out our beliefs in a way that embodies the truth. The patterns of life established by God's Word are not simply the fruit of a life well lived; they are the basis for and substance of a life well lived.

There are at least three ways we can respond very concretely and specifically to God's Word: worship, belief, and action. First, we may read a passage like Psalm 19:1-6 and be moved deeply at how the heavens declare God's glory. We might respond to this psalm by falling on our faces in worship, and this is a valid application.

Second, we may read the Word or hear a sermon preached and be convicted at the need to firm up our theology. In response to the Great Commission in Matthew 28:18-20, we might become deeply convicted about the need for all people among the nations to hear and understand the gospel.

Third, we should be characterized by hearing the Word and responding to it with concrete action. For instance, earlier I mentioned 1 Corinthians 13, the great "love chapter" among Paul's writings. In response to that chapter, we need to do more than simply say, "I need to love people more." It needs to be tangible and specific.

How do these three areas work together within your mind, heart, and will?

What are some ways you can get away to discern the "specifics" of what God is telling you?

As we follow in the steps of Christ, we need to learn to follow His instructions specifically, actively living them out step by step in our lives. We may feel handicapped spiritually in some ways, but Christ is a sure guide. By the way He has lived and by what He taught, He has shown us how to apply the truths of God's Word in tangible ways in our lives.

GROUP STUDY

Warm Up

If we are to hear and understand God's Word, we must be submissive to His will and ready to apply the Scriptures to our daily lives. In this session we look at the importance of application: how keeping God's Word is a sign that we belong to Him and why our application of God's Word should be specific and tangible. Our goal is to know God (through His Word) and to make Him known (through our witness). As you and your group discuss this final session, consider the following questions:

Can you point to specific truths of a sermon, Bible study, or time of Bible reading that you have consciously and specifically applied to your life?

In what ways have you adjusted your life in the last six months to bring your life in line with Scripture?

What role should prayer play in our study and application of the Scriptures?

What are very tangible ways that our church lives out specific applications of Scripture?

Discussion

During this time you will have an opportunity to discuss what God revealed to you during the week. Listed below are some of the questions from your daily reading assignments. They will guide your small-group discussion.

1. Why do you think Christians often focus on learning God's Word while failing to obey God's Word?

2. What makes the difference between a legalistic tradition and an authentic application of the Word?

3. What are some areas of obedience in the modern church that we tend to ignore rather than carry out? How might we change these patterns so that we are more faithful to the Word of God?

4. Why do you think John connected obedience to God's commands and our assurance of salvation?

5. What do our actions communicate about our beliefs?

6. What would it look like for us to "walk as Christ walked"?

7. What is the significance of Christ connecting love and obedience together?

8. How do these three areas (worship, belief, and action) work together within your mind, heart, and will?

9. What are some ways you can get away to discern the "specifics" of what God is telling you?

Conclusion

A few years ago, a church in Alabama was studying James. When they came to James 1:27, they read: "Pure and undefiled religion before our God and Father is this: to look after orphans and widows in their distress and to keep oneself unstained by the world." After the session, the pastor asked the leaders at the church, "Does anyone know how many orphans we have here in our county?" No one did. So the pastor called the Department of Human Resources and asked how many more foster homes would be needed to take care of all the kids who did not have a home in their county. The officials thought he was kidding and laughed at him. They would need another 150 or so families to serve as foster families.

Next, the pastor asked if the officials would come to the church and do a presentation on foster care. He called a meeting, and 162 families showed up. The people at DHR were weeping and began to ask why the church was doing this. The pastor explained their motivation to live out the Word of God in obedience. Families from the church took in all the orphans in their county. The journey wasn't easy. Some families have had challenging situations with the children they have taken into their homes. But they are living as doers of the Word, and this brings great glory to God.

Spend some time praying this for yourself and for your group:

> "God, we know everything comes from You. Grant us the ability to repent, believe, respond, and obey! Give us, through Your peace and presence, the assurance we need. Show us how to remain teachable and flexible as we do the work You have called us to do. Amen."

1. John R. W. Stott, quoted in *The Westminster Collection of Christian Quotations*, comp. Martin H. Manser (Louisville: Westminster John Knox, 2001), 19.
2. Adapted from "Hearing," by P. J. Alindogan, The Potter's Jar [online], 4 March 2012 [cited 25 September 2014]. Available from the Internet: *pottersjar.blogspot.com*.
3. See "Bible Engagement in Churchgoers' Hearts, Not Always Practiced," LifeWay Research [online], 15 November 2013 [cited 25 September 2014]. Available from the Internet: *www.lifewayresearch.com*.
4. Didymus the Blind, *Commentary on 1 John*, quoted in *James, 1–2 Peter, 1–3 John, Jude*, ed. Gerald Bray, vol. XI in *Ancient Christian Commentary on Scripture: New Testament*, 179.

The person who really loves God keeps his commandments
and by so doing realizes that he knows the love
of God. Our obedience results in his love.[4]

DIDYMUS THE BLIND

NOTES

SMALL-GROUP TIPS

Reading through this section and utilizing the suggested principles and practices will greatly enhance the group experience. First, accept your limitations. You cannot transform a life. Your group must be devoted to the Bible, the Holy Spirit, and the power of Christian community. In doing so, your group will have all the tools necessary to draw closer to God and to each other—and to experience heart transformation.

GENERAL TIPS:

- Prepare for each meeting by reviewing the material, praying for each group member, and asking the Holy Spirit to work through you as you point to Jesus each week.

- Make new attendees feel welcome.

- Think of ways to connect with group members away from group time. The amount of participation you have during your group meetings is directly related to the amount of time you connect with your group members away from the group meeting. Consider sending e-mails, texts, or social networking messages encouraging members in their personal devotion times prior to the session.

MATERIALS NEEDED:

- Bible

- Bible study book

- Pen/pencil

PROVIDE RESOURCES FOR GUESTS:

- An inexpensive way to make first-time guests feel welcome is to provide them a copy of your Bible study book. Estimate how many first-time guests you can expect during the course of your study, and secure that number of books. What about people who have not yet visited your group? You can encourage them to visit by providing a copy of the Bible study book.

SMALL-GROUP VALUES

Meeting together to study God's Word and experience life together is an exciting adventure. Here are values to consider for small-group experiences:

COMMUNITY: God is relational, so He created us to live in relationship with Him and one another. Authentic community involves sharing life together and connecting on many levels with others in our group.

INTERACTIVE BIBLE STUDY: God gave us the Bible—His great story of redeeming people from sin and death. We need to deepen our understanding of God's Word. People learn and remember more as they wrestle with truth and learn from others. Bible discovery and group interaction will enhance spiritual growth.

EXPERIENTIAL GROWTH: Beyond solely reading, studying, and dissecting the Bible, being a disciple of Christ involves marrying knowledge and experience. We do this by taking questions to God, opening a dialogue with our hearts, and utilizing other ways to listen to God speak (other people, nature, circumstances, etc.). Experiential growth is always grounded in the Bible as God's primary revelation and our ultimate truth-source.

POWER OF GOD: Processes and strategies will be ineffective unless we invite and embrace the presence and power of God. In order to experience community and growth, Jesus needs to be the centerpiece of our group experiences, and the Holy Spirit must be at work.

REDEMPTIVE COMMUNITY: Healing best occurs within the context of community and relationships. It's vital to see ourselves through the eyes of others, share our stories, and ultimately find freedom from the secrets and lies that enslave our souls.

MISSION: God has invited us into a larger story with a great mission of setting captives free and healing the broken-hearted (see Isa. 61:1-2). However, we can only join in this mission to the degree that we've let Jesus bind up our wounds and set us free. Others will be attracted to an authentic, redemptive community.